The Official West Ham United Annual 2018

WEST HAM UNITED
LONDON

Written by Rob Pritchard
Designed by Chris Dalrymple

A Grange Publication

Printed in the EU.

ISBN 978-1-911287-83-4

CONTENTS

ZABALETA
5

WEST HAM UNITED LONDON

CLARET MEMBERSHIP

BE FIRST IN LINE FOR MATCH TICKETS

- **Ticket priority** on Premier League and Cup fixtures
- **Ticket priority** on Premier League and Cup fixtures
- Access to the **Ticket Exchange** – once a fixture is sold out, you can purchase seats which have been relisted by Season Ticket Holders
- **Exclusive** prize draws
- **£5 discount** on official away coach travel
- **Exclusive** Claret Member access card
- Additional merchandise **discounts and offers**
- **Exclusive** monthly competitions - prize draws for signed
- **Exclusive** monthly competitions - prize draws for signed shirts, memorabilia and money-can't-buy experiences
- Attend PL2 matches at London Stadium **for free**
- Attend West Ham Ladies home matches **for free**

Claret Kids also get:

- Invite to **meet the players at Junior Hammers party**
- **Exclusive** gift pack including limited edition scarf, wall poster and face paint sticks

Claret Membership £40

Claret Kids Membership £25

Join today at **eticketing.co.uk/whufc** or call the Ticket Office on **0333 030 1966**

THIS ANNUAL BELONGS TO:

....

....

BIRTHDAY:

....

....

FAVOURITE WEST HAM UNITED PLAYER:

....

....

TEAM I PLAY FOR:

....

....

POSITION I PLAY:

....

....

DRAW YOUR PROFILE PICTURE:

WEST HAM UNITED
AUTOGRAPH:
SU SLAV
SUPER, SUPER SLAV
SUPER, SUPER SLAV
SUPER
SLAVEN BILIĆ!

SUPER SLAVEN BILIC!

West Ham United appointed former Hammers' defender Slaven Bilic as the Club's 15th full-time manager in June 2015.

The ex-Croatia player and manager brought his passion and knowledge of the game to east London after spells in Russia and Turkey.

Here, we find out more about the boss...

FACT FILE

Slaven Bilic

Born:
11 September 1968, Split, Croatia

Clubs played for:
Hajduk Split, Pirmorac (loan), Sibernik (loan), Karlsruher SC, West Ham United, Everton, Hajduk Split

Clubs/Nations managed:
Hajduk Split, Croatia U21, Croatia, Lokomotiv Moscow, Besiktas, West Ham United

International:
Croatia (44 caps, 3 goals)

Career Appearances/Goals:
317/29

Did You Know?
Slaven Bilic appeared for Croatia at Euro '96 and the 1998 FIFA World Cup, then managed Croatia at Euro 2008 and Euro 2012.

Won as a player
2 Croatian Cups
1 Croatian League title
1 Croatian Super Cup
1 Yugoslav Cup

Did You Know?
Slaven Bilic finished as runner-up to his present-day coaching assistant Julian Dicks for the Hammer of the Year award in 1997!

SPOT THE DIFFERENCE 1

Can you spot the ten differences between these two images of West Ham United in pre-season training in Germany?

Answers on page 59-61.

CORNERED! PABLO ZABALETA

We cornered Pablo Zabaleta with these 50/50 questions – but which options did he pick?

RIBEYE / SIRLOIN

NOEL GALLAGHER / LIAM GALLAGHER

2012 PREMIER LEAGUE TITLE / 2014 PREMIER LEAGUE TITLE

MATE / ENGLISH TEA

EASTENDERS / CORONATION STREET

LIONEL MESSI / SERGIO AGUERO

MANCHESTER DERBY / SUPERCLASICO

DIEGO MARADONA / PELE

MARIO KEMPES / GABRIEL BATISTUTA

YAYA TOURE / KOLO TOURE

GOAL / CLEAN SHEET

BOCA JUNIORS / RIVER PLATE

ROBERT DE NIRO / AL PACINO

CARLOS TEVEZ / JAVIER MASCHERANO

Answers on page 59-61.

YOU'RE THE MANAGER

Every supporter believes they could manage West Ham United – and now you get your chance! Using the formation below and the players on the opposite page, select your Hammers starting XI and three substitutes to challenge the best!

GOALKEEPER

GK: Phill Parkes

DEFENDERS

D: Bobbymo[illegible]

D: Billy Bonds

D: Alvin martin

D: Rio Ferdinand

MIDFIELDERS

M: Brooking

M: antonio

M: noble

M: lanzini

FORWARDS

F: Hurst

F: Di canio

SUBS

Green | Potts | Joe Cole | Teves | Clarton Cole

GOALKEEPERS

Ludek Miklosko

Joe Hart

Robert Green

Phil Parkes

DEFENDERS

Bobby Moore

Billy Bonds

Julian Dicks

Alvin Martin

Rio Ferdinand

Winston Reid

James Collins

Steve Potts

MIDFIELDERS

Trevor Brooking

Joe Cole

Michail Antonio

Mark Noble

Scott Parker

Martin Peters

Alan Devonshire

Manuel Lanzini

FORWARDS

Geoff Hurst

Paolo Di Canio

Carlos Tevez

Carlton Cole

Chicharito

Tony Cottee

11 THINGS YOU PROBABLY DIDN'T KNOW ABOUT WEST HAM UNITED!

1 West Ham United has not always been called West Ham United. Between 1895 and 1900, the Club was named Thames Ironworks Football Club!

2 West Ham United played in the first-ever FA Cup final at Wembley Stadium in 1923 in front of an estimated 300,000 fans. Unfortunately, they saw the Hammers lose 2-0 to Bolton Wanderers...

3 Nobody has netted more goals for West Ham United than the amazing Vic Watson, who scored 326 times between 1920 and 1935. Beat that!

4 Bobby Moore captained West Ham United to the FA Cup in 1964 and European Cup Winners' Cup in 1965, then England to the FIFA World Cup in 1966. What a hat-trick!

5 Sir Trevor Brooking won five Hammer of the Year awards between 1972 and 1984 – more than any other player!

6 West Ham United have won the FA Cup three times – 1964, 1975 and 1980.

7 Billy Bonds made an amazing 799 appearances for West Ham United between 1967 and 1988 – 129 more than any other player!

8 Strikers Frank McAvennie and Tony Cottee scored 46 goals between them as the Hammers finished third in Division One in 1985/86. That's a club record!

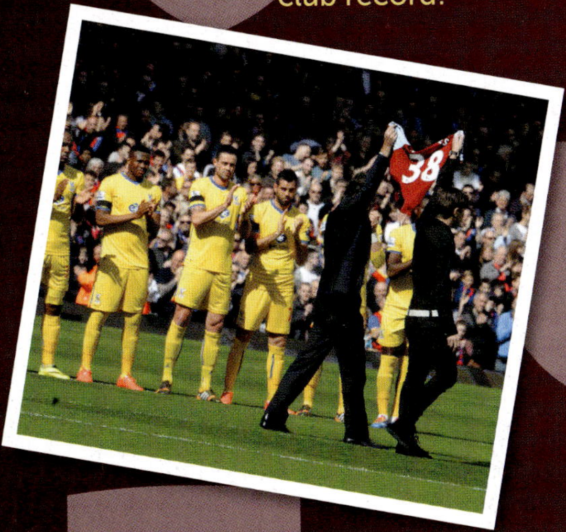

9 The Club has retired two numbers – Bobby Moore's No6 and the No38 worn by the late Dylan Tombides.

10 West Ham United's record home attendance is the 56,996 who attended the Premier League game with Manchester United on 2 January 2017.

11 West Ham United were named in Forbes' list of the world's 20 most valuable football clubs in 2015, 2016 and 2017!

GOALKEEPERS

ADRIAN

DATE OF BIRTH: 3 JANUARY 1987

PLACE OF BIRTH: SEVILLE, SPAIN

HEIGHT: 1.9M

JOINED WEST HAM UNITED: JULY 2013 FROM REAL BETIS

WEST HAM UNITED APPEARANCES: 123

WEST HAM UNITED CLEAN SHEETS: 33

DID YOU KNOW? ADRIAN RECEIVED HIS FIRST CALL-UP TO THE SENIOR SPAIN SQUAD IN AUGUST 2016

FIFA17 RATING: 80

JOE HART

DATE OF BIRTH: 19 APRIL 1987

PLACE OF BIRTH: SHREWSBURY, ENGLAND

HEIGHT: 1.96M

JOINED WEST HAM UNITED: JULY 2017 FROM MANCHESTER CITY

WEST HAM UNITED APPEARANCES: 0

WEST HAM UNITED CLEAN SHEETS: 0

DID YOU KNOW? UP UNTIL JUNE 2017, JOE HART HAD KEPT GOAL IN 43 OF ENGLAND'S PREVIOUS 45 COMPETITIVE INTERNATIONALS

FIFA17 RATING: 84

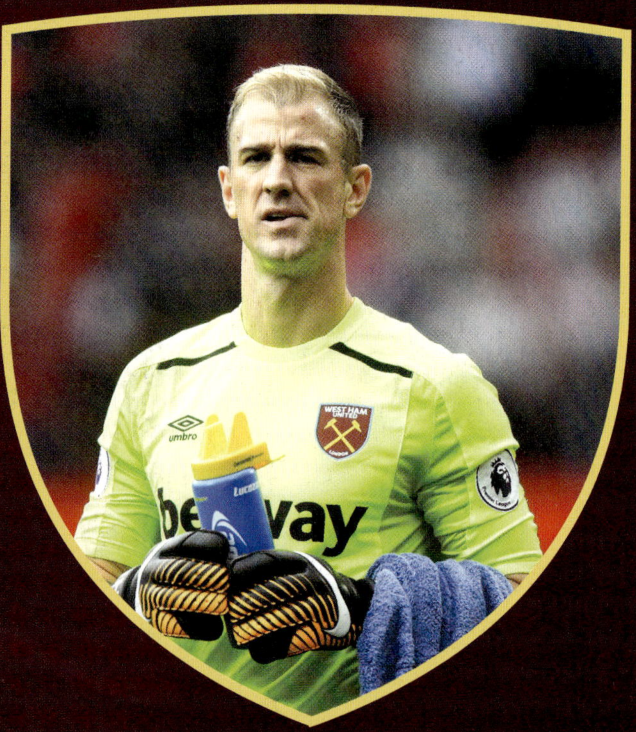

NATHAN TROTT

DATE OF BIRTH: 21 NOVEMBER 1998

PLACE OF BIRTH: BERMUDA

HEIGHT: 1.93M

JOINED WEST HAM UNITED: JANUARY 2016

WEST HAM UNITED APPEARANCES: 0

WEST HAM UNITED CLEAN SHEETS: 0

DID YOU KNOW? ORIGINALLY A WINGER, NATHAN TROTT WAS CONVERTED TO A GOALKEEPER AND TRAVELLED WITH ENGLAND TO THE 2017 UEFA U19 CHAMPIONSHIP FINALS

FIFA17 RATING: N/A

RIHARDS MATREVICS

DATE OF BIRTH: 18 MARCH 1999

PLACE OF BIRTH: LATVIA

HEIGHT: 2.0M

JOINED WEST HAM UNITED: SEPTEMBER 2015

WEST HAM UNITED APPEARANCES: 0

WEST HAM UNITED CLEAN SHEETS: 0

DID YOU KNOW? RIHARDS MATREVICS IS A FILM BUFF, NAMING THE EQUALISER AND THE BOURNE SERIES AS HIS FAVOURITE MOVIES!

FIFA17 RATING: N/A

NAME THE HAMMER – PICTURE QUIZ

How well do you know your former Hammers? These 15 players have all played for West Ham United since 2012, but can you name them? Give yourself one point for each correct answer!

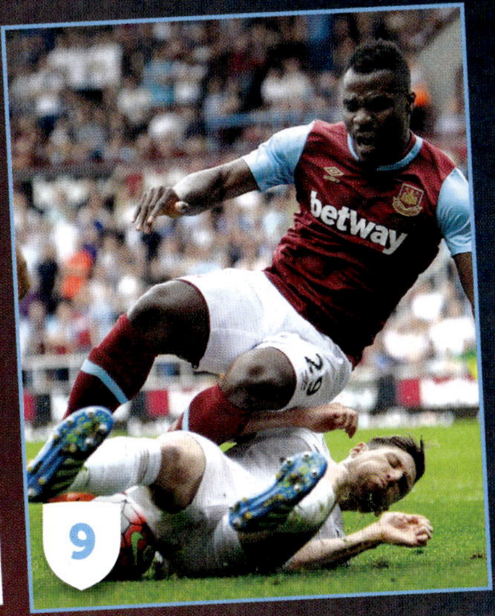

Payet

Answers on page 59-61.

WEST HAM UNITED
LONDON
ANTONIO
ANTONIO!
ANTONIO...
AUTOGRAPH:

CORNERED! AARON CRESSWELL

We cornered Aaron Cresswell with these 50/50 questions – but which options did he pick?

XBOX / PS4

SUSHI / PASTA

FERRARI / LAMBORGHINI

LOUISA JOHNSON / PIXIE LOTT

TEA / COFFEE

FA CUP WINNER / UEFA CHAMPIONS LEAGUE PLACE

LIONEL MESSI / CRISTIANO RONALDO

DOGS / CATS

SNAPCHAT / INSTAGRAM

PELE / DIEGO MARADONA

BEACH HOLIDAY / CITY BREAK

X FACTOR / THE VOICE

KEVIN KEEGAN / KENNY DALGLISH

STEVEN GERRARD / FRANK LAMPARD

Answers on page 59-61.

MATCH THE FACT TO THE HAMMER!

Find out how much you know about your favourite West Ham United players. You get one point for every correct answer!

1 I made my England debut in Trinidad & Tobago in 2008 and now have more than 70 caps.

2 I scored West Ham United's first-ever goal at London Stadium.

3 I have played for both Turin-based clubs in Italy's Serie A.

4 I scored a hat-trick for Scotland in Malta in September 2016.

5 I was born in Sweden but play international football for Montenegro.

6 I'm one of just 19 Hammers to have made more than 400 appearances for the Club.

7 I've won league titles in Argentina and Brazil.

8 I played 70 games in League One and 132 in the Championship before I joined West Ham United.

9 I won back-to-back Superleague Greece titles in 2015 and 2016.

10 I won my 50th international cap for Wales against Moldova in September 2016.

11 I started my career with non-league club Tooting & Mitcham United.

12 My father Manolo runs a fruit and vegetable stall in a market in my home city of Seville.

13 My cousins played in the Premier League for Sunderland and Manchester City.

14 I captained West Ham United's U23s to Premier League 2 promotion last season.

15 I scored my first competitive goal for Newcastle United against West Ham United!

16 My father was named African Footballer of the Year three times!

17 I played four times for my country as we won UEFA Euro 2016.

18 I scored in two different Wembley finals for Barnsley in 2016.

19 I won the 2005 World Youth Championship playing alongside Lionel Messi and Sergio Aguero.

20 I scored my first West Ham United goal at Southampton in February 2017.

Answers on page 59-61.

AUTOGRAPH:
MARK NOBLE... WHOOAAOO!
MARK NOBLE... WHOOAAOO!
HE'S WEST HAM THROUGH AND THROUGH, HE PLAYS FOR THE CLARET AND BLUE!

DEFENDERS

WINSTON REID

DATE OF BIRTH: 3 JULY 1988
PLACE OF BIRTH: AUCKLAND, NEW ZEALAND
HEIGHT: 1.9M
JOINED WEST HAM UNITED: AUGUST 2010 FROM FC MIDTJYLLAND
WEST HAM UNITED APPEARANCES: 203
WEST HAM UNITED CLEAN SHEETS: 55
DID YOU KNOW? WINSTON REID IS ONE OF ONLY FOUR NEW ZEALANDERS TO SCORE AT A FIFA WORLD CUP FINAL – HE NETTED AGAINST SLOVAKIA AT SOUTH AFRICA 2010
FIFA17 RATING: 84

AARON CRESSWELL

DATE OF BIRTH: 15 DECEMBER 1989
PLACE OF BIRTH: LIVERPOOL, ENGLAND
HEIGHT: 1.7M
JOINED WEST HAM UNITED: JULY 2014 FROM IPSWICH TOWN
WEST HAM UNITED APPEARANCES: 124
WEST HAM UNITED CLEAN SHEETS: 28
DID YOU KNOW? AARON CRESSWELL BECAME WEST HAM UNITED'S 40TH FULL ENGLAND INTERNATIONAL WHEN HE MADE HIS DEBUT AGAINST SPAIN IN NOVEMBER 2016
FIFA17 RATING: 76

PABLO ZABALETA

DATE OF BIRTH: 16 JANUARY 1985
PLACE OF BIRTH: ARRECIFES, ARGENTINA
HEIGHT: 1.74M
JOINED WEST HAM UNITED: JULY 2017 FROM MANCHESTER CITY
WEST HAM UNITED APPEARANCES: 0
WEST HAM UNITED CLEAN SHEETS: 0
DID YOU KNOW? PABLO ZABALETA HAS WON THE PREMIER LEAGUE, FA CUP, EFL CUP, SPANISH CUP, COPA SUDAMERICANA, FIFA U-20 WORLD CUP AND AN OLYMPIC GOLD MEDAL
FIFA17 RATING: 82

DEFENDERS

JAMES COLLINS

DATE OF BIRTH: 23 AUGUST 1983
PLACE OF BIRTH: NEWPORT, WALES
HEIGHT: 1.88M
JOINED WEST HAM UNITED: AUGUST 2012 FROM ASTON VILLA
WEST HAM UNITED APPEARANCES: 199
WEST HAM UNITED CLEAN SHEETS: 54
DID YOU KNOW? JAMES COLLINS WAS PART OF THE WALES SQUAD WHICH REACHED THE SEMI-FINALS OF UEFA EURO 2016
FIFA17 RATING: 76

ANGELO OGBONNA

DATE OF BIRTH: 23 MAY 1988
PLACE OF BIRTH: CASSINO, ITALY
HEIGHT: 1.91M
JOINED WEST HAM UNITED: JULY 2015 FROM JUVENTUS
WEST HAM UNITED APPEARANCES: 60
WEST HAM UNITED CLEAN SHEETS: 16
DID YOU KNOW? ANGELO OGBONNA WAS PART OF THE ITALY SQUAD WHICH FINISHED AS RUNNERS-UP AT UEFA EURO 2012
FIFA17 RATING: 80

SAM BYRAM

DATE OF BIRTH: 16 SEPTEMBER 1993
PLACE OF BIRTH: THURROCK, ENGLAND
HEIGHT: 1.8M
JOINED WEST HAM UNITED: JANUARY 2016 FROM LEEDS UNITED
WEST HAM UNITED APPEARANCES: 26
WEST HAM UNITED CLEAN SHEETS: 5
DID YOU KNOW? SAM BYRAM MADE HIS WEST HAM UNITED DEBUT AGAINST PREMIER LEAGUE CHAMPIONS MANCHESTER CITY AT THE BOLEYN GROUND ON 20 JANUARY 2016
FIFA17 RATING: 73

JOSE FONTE

DATE OF BIRTH: 22 DECEMBER 1983
PLACE OF BIRTH: PENAFIEL, PORTUGAL
HEIGHT: 1.87M
JOINED WEST HAM UNITED: JANUARY 2017 FROM SOUTHAMPTON
WEST HAM UNITED APPEARANCES: 16
WEST HAM UNITED CLEAN SHEETS: 4
DID YOU KNOW? JOSE FONTE AND MICHAIL ANTONIO WERE BOTH PART OF THE SOUTHAMPTON TEAM WHICH WON THE FOOTBALL LEAGUE TROPHY IN 2010
FIFA17 RATING: 83

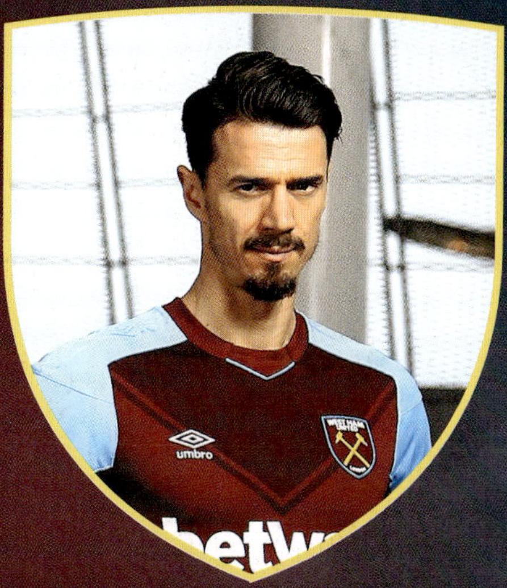

ARTHUR MASUAKU

DATE OF BIRTH: 7 NOVEMBER 1993
PLACE OF BIRTH: LILLE, FRANCE
HEIGHT: 1.79M
JOINED WEST HAM UNITED: AUGUST 2016 FROM OLYMPIACOS
WEST HAM UNITED APPEARANCES: 15
WEST HAM UNITED CLEAN SHEETS: 4
DID YOU KNOW? OF THE 50 SUPERLEAGUE GREECE APPEARANCES ARTHUR MASUAKU MADE FOR OLYMPIACOS, HE LOST JUST FIVE!
FIFA17 RATING: 75

DECLAN RICE

DATE OF BIRTH: 14 JANUARY 1999
PLACE OF BIRTH: LONDON, ENGLAND
HEIGHT: 1.85M
JOINED WEST HAM UNITED: ACADEMY OF FOOTBALL
WEST HAM UNITED APPEARANCES: 1
WEST HAM UNITED CLEAN SHEETS: 0
DID YOU KNOW? DECLAN RICE WAS CALLED-UP TO THE REPUBLIC OF IRELAND SENIOR SQUAD FOR THE FIRST TIME IN MAY 2017, AGED 18
FIFA17 RATING: 56

BUBBLES AND HAMMERHEAD'S ANNUAL TEASERS!

CREATED BY ALEX BENNETT - WWW.ROUNDHEADILLUSTRATION.COM

THE TWO GRIDS BELOW IS DIVIDED INTO FOUR SECTIONS. YOUR JOB IS TO HAVE EACH OF THE FOUR ITEMS APPEAR ONCE IN EACH SECTION AND IN EACH ROW AND COLUMN.

FILL EACH SQUARE WITH THE ITEM'S IMAGE OR THEIR NAME.

NO ITEM CAN REPEAT IN ANY SECTION, ROW, OR COLUMN.

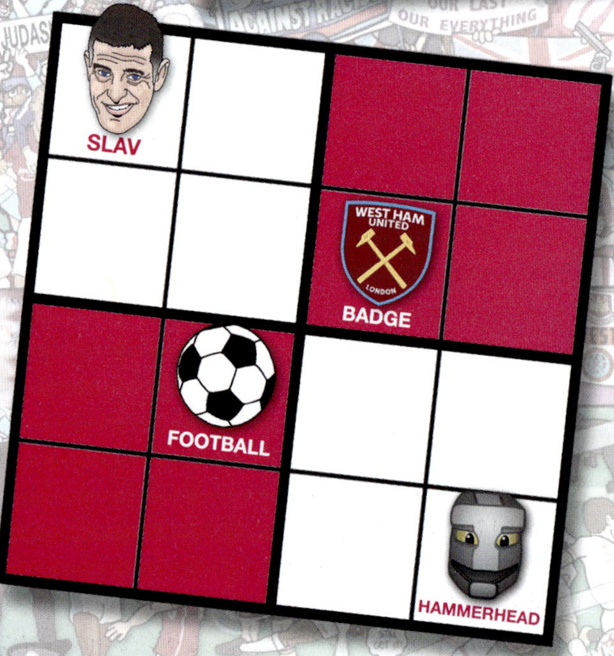

ANDY CARROLL WON OUR 2016/17 GOAL OF THE SEASON WITH A SPECTACULAR BICYCLE KICK.

1. Which London club were our opposition that day?

A Crystal Palace

B Chelsea

C Arsenal

2. Which player crossed the ball for Carroll?

A André Ayew

B Michail Antonio

C Aaron Cresswell

3. What was the final score?

A 1-0   B 1-1   C 3-0

GROUNDED

Which Premier League club play here?

....

Grid Solution:

BUBBLES' TRICKY TEASER

What number do you get if you add up our final league position from the last three seasons?

A 26

B 30

C 34

Answers:

Bubbles' Tricky Teaser: (B) 30. 2014/15 - 12th. 2015/16 - 7th. 2016/17 - 11th.

Andy Carroll's goal: 1. (A) Crystal Palace

2. (B) Michail Antonio 3. (C) 3-0

Grounded: Huddersfield Town

WEST HAM UNITED FAMOUS FANS XI

The Hammers have attracted dozens of celebrity supporters over the years. We have selected a Famous Fans XI ready to take on all-comers – what do you think?

LOUISA JOHNSON

Essex-born Louisa Johnson won The X Factor in 2015 and sang live at Mark Noble's Testimonial in February 2016.

PIXIE LOTT

Singer and actress Pixie Lott has been spotted regularly wearing a Claret and Blue shirt and performed at London Stadium in April 2017.

GENNADY GOLOVKIN

Kazakhstani professional boxer Gennady Golovkin – nicknamed GGG – is an unbeaten middleweight world champion and personal friend of Joint-Chairman David Sullivan.

BEN SHEPHARD

Born and raised in Epping, television presenter Ben Shephard is a lifelong Hammer and regular participant in the annual Soccer Aid charity football match.

RAY WINSTONE

Hollywood star Ray Winstone is never shy to share his loud and proud love for all things West Ham United.

JAMES CORDEN

Award-winning actor, comedian and television host is a lifelong Hammer and regular visitor at West Ham United matches.

DANNY DYER

Canning Town-born Danny Dyer's art has imitated life in his role of Mick Carter in the long-running soap opera EastEnders.

STEPHEN MOYER

Actor and director Stephen Moyer is best known for his role as vampire Bill Compton in the hit HBO series True Blood.

STEVE HARRIS

One to ask your Dad about! Steve Harris is the bassist in the legendary heavy metal band Iron Maiden.

RUSSELL BRAND

Comedian, broadcaster and author Russell Brand has developed a reputation for kissing West Ham United managers during their post-match interviews!

TRIPLE H

WWE superstar Triple H loves West Ham United's worth ethic and has visited both the Boleyn Ground and London Stadium.

SOCK
AIN'T NOBODY, LIKE
LANZINI
MAKES US HAPPY,
PLAYS THE
WEST HAM WAY!
AUTOGRAPH:

We Are West Ham's Claret and Blue Army
HOME KIT 2017/18
AVAILABLE IN ALL OFFICIAL STORES AND ONLINE
officialwesthamstore.com
STADIUM STORE | LONDON E20 2ST
THE LIBERTY ROMFORD | ROMFORD RM1 3RL
LAKESIDE THURROCK | ESSEX RM20 2ZG

FUTURE STARS

West Ham United's Academy of Football has been synonymous with producing top-class players for more than 50 years, including the likes of Bobby Moore, Martin Peters, Paul Ince, Rio Ferdinand, Frank Lampard, Joe Cole and Mark Noble. Will any of these ten bright young things follow in their footsteps and become full internationals? Only time will tell.

Tunji Akinola

Born: **21 November 1998**

Position: **Defender**

An athletic centre-back, Tunji Akinola's maturity saw him selected for West Ham United U18s at the age of 15 and later be named captain of the youth team.

Kristijan Belic

Born: 25 March 2001

Position: Midfield

Serbian defensive midfielder Kristijan Belic joined West Ham United as a schoolboy before signing a two-year scholarship in summer 2017.

Conor Coventry

Born: 25 March 2000

Position: Midfield

Republic of Ireland U17 international Conor Coventry scored in the first-ever Premier League 2 fixture at London Stadium, a 2-0 win over Fulham in February 2017.

Grady Diangana

Born: 19 March 1998

Position: Winger

A creative talent, Grady Diangana can play on either wing or as a central attacking midfielder, positions he filled as the U23s gained Premier League 2 promotion in 2017.

Anouar El Mhassani

Born: 18 April 2001

Position: Midfield

Left-sided Dutch attacking midfielder/winger Anouar El Mhassani joined West Ham United after spending eight years with Amsterdam giants Ajax.

Jahmal Hector-Ingram

Born: 11 November 1998

Position: Striker

Capped by England at U16 level, prolific centre-forward Jahmal Hector-Ingram has long been considered one of the Academy's brightest attacking prospects.

Nathan Holland

Born: 19 June 1998

Position: Winger

England U19 international Nathan Holland joined West Ham United on a three-and-a-half year contract in January 2017, having spent the formative years of his career with Everton.

Dan Kemp

Born: 11 January 1999

Position: Winger

Diminutive Dan Kemp joined West Ham United from Chelsea in November 2015. He has since helped the Hammers win the Premier League Cup and England U20s to victory at the Toulon Tournament.

Vashon Neufville

Born: 18 July 1999

Position: Left-back

Like Dan Kemp, full-back Vashon Neufville spent time with Chelsea before moving across London as an U14. He has since been a regular starter at U18, U21 and U23 levels.

Joe Powell

Born: 30 October 1998

Position: Central midfield

The younger brother of former Hammers youngster Jack, Joe Powell is a talented two-footed midfielder who has the vision and ability to open up the tightest of defences.

SPOT THE DIFFERENCE 2

Can you find the ten differences between these two images of West Ham United?

Answers on page 59-61.

COLOURING TIME

It's time to grab your crayons or colouring pencils and show off your artistic side by colouring in this drawing of Chicharito! Don't forget to pick the correct colours and keep within the lines. Good luck!

BY THE NUMBERS

Football is all about numbers! Who has scored the most goals? Who has made the most appearances? Who were the youngest and oldest players to wear a Claret and Blue shirt? Here, you can find out more about West Ham United's record breakers!

1,124

Syd King managed more West Ham United matches than anyone else. He was in charge for 30 years between 1902 and 1932!

289

At the end of the 2016/17 season, Mark Noble had made more Premier League appearances than anyone else. Carlton Cole in second place played 73 games fewer.

799

Billy Bonds played more matches for West Ham United than anyone else between 1967 and 1988. Bonds lifted the FA Cup twice and retired at the age of 41!

3

West Ham United have won the FA Cup on three occasions, in 1964, 1975 and 1980.

5

Julian Dicks and Steve Lomas are West Ham United's all-time biggest bad boys – both were sent-off five times in a Hammers shirt!

326

Nobody has scored – or will likely ever score – as many goals for West Ham United than Vic Watson, who netted an average of 22 every season between 1920 and 1935.

5

Trevor Brooking played for West Ham United, managed West Ham United and was also voted Hammer of the Year a record five times!

111

Carlton Cole was introduced as a substitute in 111 of his 293 appearances for the Hammers – more than twice as many times as second place Bobby Zamora's 52.

16

years and 198 days Reece Oxford became West Ham United's youngest-ever player when he faced Lusitans of Andorra in the UEFA Europa League in July 2015, breaking Billy Williams' 93-year-old record.

68

Vic Watson might be West Ham United's all-time goal king, but it is Geoff Hurst who has scored more cup goals than any other Hammer in history!

38

years and 128 days At the other end of the age spectrum, Teddy Sheringham became West Ham United's oldest debutant when he faced Leicester City in the Championship in August 2004.

10-0

Tony Cottee scored four goals in West Ham United's all-time record victory, which came against Bury in the League Cup second round in October 1983.

59,996

West Ham United's all-time record attendance came as recently as 2 January 2017, when Manchester United visited London Stadium in the Premier League.

MIDFIELDERS

CHEIKHOU KOUYATE

DATE OF BIRTH: 21 DECEMBER 1989
PLACE OF BIRTH: DAKAR, SENEGAL
HEIGHT: 1.89M
JOINED WEST HAM UNITED: JUNE 2014 FROM ANDERLECHT
WEST HAM UNITED APPEARANCES: 110
WEST HAM UNITED GOALS: 13
DID YOU KNOW? CHEIKHOU KOUYATE SCORED THE FIRST TWO GOALS AT LONDON STADIUM IN THE HAMMERS' UEFA EUROPA LEAGUE WIN OVER DOMZALE IN JULY 2016
FIFA17 RATING: 77

MANUEL LANZINI

DATE OF BIRTH: 15 FEBRUARY 1993
PLACE OF BIRTH: ITUZAINGO PARTIDO, ARGENTINA
HEIGHT: 1.67M
JOINED WEST HAM UNITED: JULY 2015 FROM AL JAZIRA CLUB
WEST HAM UNITED APPEARANCES: 70
WEST HAM UNITED CLEAN SHEETS: 15
DID YOU KNOW? MANUEL LANZINI SCORED JUST TWO MINUTES INTO HIS WEST HAM UNITED DEBUT AGAINST ROMANIAN CLUB ASTRA GIURGIU IN AUGUST 2015
FIFA17 RATING: 83

ROBERT SNODGRASS

DATE OF BIRTH: 7 SEPTEMBER 1987
PLACE OF BIRTH: GLASGOW, SCOTLAND
HEIGHT: 1.82M
JOINED WEST HAM UNITED: JANUARY 2017 FROM HULL CITY
WEST HAM UNITED APPEARANCES: 15
WEST HAM UNITED CLEAN SHEETS: 0
DID YOU KNOW? ROBERT SNODGRASS SCORED SCOTLAND'S FIRST COMPETITIVE HAT-TRICK IN NEARLY 50 YEARS AGAINST MALTA IN SEPTEMBER 2016
FIFA17 RATING: 75

PEDRO OBIANG

DATE OF BIRTH: 27 MARCH 1992
PLACE OF BIRTH: ALCALA DE HENARES, SPAIN
HEIGHT: 1.85M
JOINED WEST HAM UNITED: JUNE 2015 FROM SAMPDORIA
WEST HAM UNITED APPEARANCES: 60
WEST HAM UNITED CLEAN SHEETS: 1
DID YOU KNOW? PEDRO OBIANG SCORED HIS FIRST WEST HAM UNITED GOAL IN A 3-1 PREMIER LEAGUE WIN AT SOUTHAMPTON ON 4 FEBRUARY 2017
FIFA17 RATING: 76

MARK NOBLE

DATE OF BIRTH: 8 MAY 1987
PLACE OF BIRTH: CANNING TOWN, LONDON, ENGLAND
HEIGHT: 1.8M
JOINED WEST HAM UNITED: ACADEMY OF FOOTBALL
WEST HAM UNITED APPEARANCES: 402
WEST HAM UNITED CLEAN SHEETS: 47
DID YOU KNOW? MARK NOBLE HAS WON THE HAMMER OF THE YEAR AWARD AND BEEN PROMOTED TO THE PREMIER LEAGUE ON TWO OCCASIONS
FIFA17 RATING: 78

MICHAIL ANTONIO

DATE OF BIRTH: 28 MARCH 1990
PLACE OF BIRTH: WANDSWORTH, LONDON, ENGLAND
HEIGHT: 1.8M
JOINED WEST HAM UNITED: SEPTEMBER 2015 FROM NOTTINGHAM FOREST
WEST HAM UNITED APPEARANCES: 69
WEST HAM UNITED CLEAN SHEETS: 18
DID YOU KNOW? MICHAIL ANTONIO WON THE COVETED HAMMER OF THE YEAR AWARD AT THE END OF THE 2016/17 SEASON
FIFA17 RATING: 82

MIDFIELDERS

EDIMILSON FERNANDES

DATE OF BIRTH: 15 APRIL 1996
PLACE OF BIRTH: SION, SWITZERLAND
HEIGHT: 1.9M
JOINED WEST HAM UNITED: AUGUST 2016 FROM FC SION
WEST HAM UNITED APPEARANCES: 32
WEST HAM UNITED CLEAN SHEETS: 1
DID YOU KNOW? EDIMILSON FERNANDES SCORED IN FC SION'S 3-0 VICTORY OVER FC BASEL IN THE FINAL OF THE 2015 SWISS CUP

SEAD HAKSABANOVIC

DATE OF BIRTH: 4 MAY 1999
PLACE OF BIRTH: HYLTEBRUK, SWEDEN
HEIGHT: 1.74M
JOINED WEST HAM UNITED: AUGUST 2017 FROM HALMSTADS BK
WEST HAM UNITED APPEARANCES: 0
WEST HAM UNITED CLEAN SHEETS: 0
DID YOU KNOW? SEAD HAKSABANOVIC BECAME THE SECOND-YOUNGEST PLAYER IN SWEDISH LEAGUE HISTORY WHEN HE DEBUTED AGAINST IFK NORRKOPING IN APRIL 2015
FIFA17 RATING: 54

MARKO ARNAUTOVIC

DATE OF BIRTH: 19 APRIL 1989
PLACE OF BIRTH: FLORIDSDORF, AUSTRIA
HEIGHT: 1.92M
JOINED WEST HAM UNITED: ACADEMY OF FOOTBALL
WEST HAM UNITED APPEARANCES: 0
WEST HAM UNITED CLEAN SHEETS: 0
DID YOU KNOW? MARKO ARNAUTOVIC MADE HIS INTERNATIONAL DEBUT FOR AUSTRIA IN OCTOBER 2008 AND HAS BEEN CAPPED IN EVERY CALENDAR YEAR SINCE
FIFA17 RATING: 82

SOCIAL HAMMERS

You can follow your favourite West Ham United stars on social media. Here's a guide to the accounts which give you the inside story, direct from your Hammers' smartphones!

Player	Instagram	Twitter
Winston Reid	@winston.reid2	@WinstonReid2
Aaron Cresswell	@cresser3	@Aaron_Cresswell
Jose Fonte	@f6nte	
Pablo Zabaleta		@pablo_zabaleta
Marko Arnautovic	@arnautovic_10	
Cheikhou Kouyate	@roilionpapis8	@PapiCheikhou
Andy Carroll	@andytcarroll	@AndyTCarroll
Manuel Lanzini	@manulanzini	@maanuulanzini10
Robert Snodgrass	@snods_10	@robsnodgrass7
Adrian	@adr13nsanmiguel	@AdriSanMiguel
Pedro Obiang	@pedrombaobiang	@Obiang14
Diafra Sakho	@iamdiafrasakho	@iamdiafrasakho
Mark Noble	@nobes2122	@Noble16Mark
Chicharito	@ch14_instagram	@CH14_
James Collins	@gingercollins19	
Andre Ayew	@andreayew10	@AyewAndre
Angelo Ogbonna	@angeloogbonna21	@OgbonnaOfficial
Sam Byram	@sambyram93	@sambyram93
Sead Haksabanovic	@seadhaksabanovic	@seadhaksabanovic
Joe Hart	@joehartofficial	
Arthur Masuaku	@masuaku26	@ArthurMasuaku
Michail Antonio	@antonio_michail	@Michailantonio
Edimilson Fernandes	@e.fernandes31	
Declan Rice		@_DeclanRice

ALL-TIME GREATS

More than 900 players have pulled on a West Ham United shirt since the Club's formation at Thames Ironworks FC in 1895.

From great goalkeepers to defiant defenders and mercurial midfielders to sensational strikers, the Hammers have fielded fantastic players in every position.

Here, we meet seven of the very best...

BILLY BONDS

Born: 17 September 1946

Honours: FA Cup (1975, 1980), Second Division (1980/81)

Individual: Hammer of the Year (1971, 1974, 1975, 1987), First Division Team of the Year (1974/75), Second Division Team of the Year (1979/80, 1980/81)

Appearances/Goals: 799/61

MARTIN PETERS

Born: 8 November 1943

Honours: FIFA World Cup (1966), FA Cup (1964), UEFA Cup Winners' Cup (1965)

Individual: Hammer of the Year (1965)

Appearances/Goals: 364/100

International: England (67 caps, 20 goals)

TREVOR BROOKING

Born: 2 October 1948

Honours: FA Cup (1975, 1980), Second Division (1980/81)

Individual: Hammer of the Year (1972, 1976, 1977, 1978, 1984), First Division Team of the Year (1976/77, 1977/78), Second Division Team of the Year (1978/79, 1979/80, 1980/81)

Appearances/Goals: 643/102

International: England (47 caps, 5 goals)

VIC WATSON

Born: 10 November 1897

Died: 3 August 1988

Honours: British Home Championship (1930)

Appearances/Goals: 505/326

International: England (5 caps, 4 goals)

GEOFF HURST

Born: 8 December 1941

Honours: FIFA World Cup (1966), FA Cup (1964), UEFA Cup Winners' Cup (1965)

Individual: Hammer of the Year (1966, 1967, 1969)

Appearances/Goals: 503/249

International: England (49 caps, 24 goals)

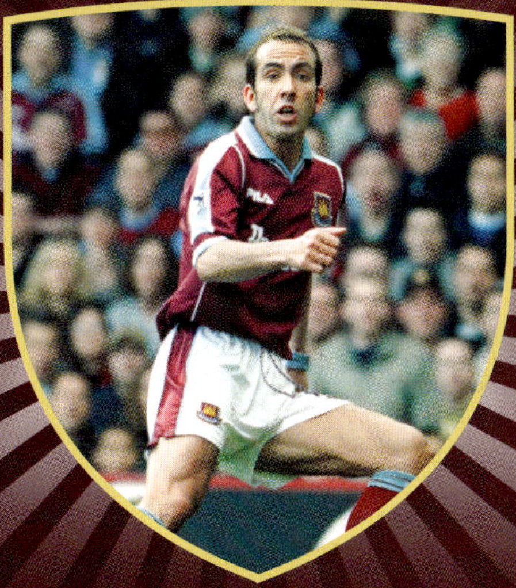

PAOLO DI CANIO

Born: 9 July 1968

Honours: UEFA Intertoto Cup (1999)

Individual: Hammer of the Year (2000), Match of the Day Goal of the Season (1999/00), FIFA Fair Play Award (2001)

Appearances/Goals: 141/51

International: Italy B (1 cap)

BOBBY MOORE

Born: 12 April 1941

Died: 24 February 1993

Honours: FIFA World Cup (1966), FA Cup (1964), UEFA Cup Winners' Cup (1965)

Individual: Hammer of the Year (1961, 1963, 1968, 1970), Footballer of the Year (1964), BBC Sports Personality of the Year (1966)

Appearances/Goals: 647/27

International: England (108 caps, 2 goals)

MICHAIL ANTONIO'S CELEBRATION MASTERCLASS

Michail Antonio has scored some memorable goals since joining West Ham United in August 2015 – and he has followed them with some equally memorable celebrations! Here, the winger gives you the lowdown on how to recreate his eye-catching moves...

THE HOMER SIMPSON

This is one that was inspired by the cartoon character Homer Simpson. You need to get down and dirty to do the Homer! You need to get down on the ground and lay on your side and then do the Running Man in a circle. Keep going until you can't run any longer, or until your teammates come to celebrate with you!

THE CARLTON BANKS

You might be too young to know who Carlton Banks is, so I'll explain! He was a character from a comedy show called The Fresh Prince of Bel Air, which also starred Will Smith, and he was famous for his funky dance moves. To do the Carlton, which is a nice little move, you need to sway your hips, bend your arms and click your fingers!

THE HAMMERS HAKA

This was a move that I did after being challenged by a supporter on Twitter! The Haka is a traditional war dance that is used by the Maori people of New Zealand. I put together my own take and used it after I scored against Stoke City at London Stadium – I hope you liked it!

THE MACARENA

This is another dance which most of you are definitely too young to remember! The Macarena was a dance craze which was introduced by a Spanish group called Los Del Rio in the mid-1990s! It's a fairly complicated dance, but essentially you need to move your arms, your hips and jump around a lot!

THE WORM

The Worm is an absolute classic dance move which dates back to the 1970s and 1980s, before even I was born! Basically, you need to lie on the pitch on your front, then shift your weight from your upper body to lower body – or vice versa – and push off the ground using your hands so you move forwards and backwards like a worm!

We All Follow The West Ham
betway
umbro
WEST HAM UNITED LONDON
AWAY KIT
2017/18
AVAILABLE IN ALL OFFICIAL STORES AND ONLINE
officialwesthamstore.com
STADIUM STORE | LONDON E20 2ST
THE LIBERTY ROMFORD | ROMFORD RM1 3RL
LAKESIDE THURROCK | ESSEX RM20 2ZG

WORDSEARCH

Can you find the following West Ham United-related words and phrases hiding in our wordsearch? (Answers on page 59-61)

R	J	S	L	N	M	K	R	F	Z	M	Y	M	T	Z	L	W	D
Y	J	R	E	R	N	L	W	E	K	N	K	B	K	V	V	O	E
N	T	B	K	L	K	P	V	P	B	O	L	E	Y	N	N	V	T
F	U	R	B	R	B	E	N	O	B	L	E	R	L	B	M	E	I
M	O	O	V	S	T	B	P	Y	B	G	J	Q	R	T	G	R	N
V	H	O	N	N	T	J	U	K	T	L	J	B	V	D	F	L	U
K	S	K	P	K	M	R	T	B	C	R	U	G	D	J	Q	A	M
N	D	I	X	X	R	K	A	H	C	K	A	E	F	M	V	N	A
T	N	N	R	T	G	G	I	T	M	X	C	H	K	R	K	D	H
J	A	G	V	H	Z	C	N	R	F	P	E	T	E	R	S	A	T
H	T	H	F	H	H	N	E	R	O	O	M	N	J	O	L	N	S
J	S	V	G	A	O	S	D	K	F	P	R	F	L	M	J	D	E
J	I	C	R	D	R	I	B	Q	R	M	V	D	N	B	Z	S	W
P	W	I	N	E	C	W	O	Z	B	L	Y	M	H	K	T	E	F
R	T	O	M	A	I	H	N	N	Q	P	M	V	W	Y	K	A	Z
O	L	M	N	K	L	N	D	N	C	P	T	E	R	A	L	C	L
T	A	I	B	K	I	N	S	V	K	K	L	R	W	N	K	R	Z
H	O	M	N	L	B	P	F	B	L	B	D	R	R	T	Z	D	H

CLARET MOORE DI CANIO CHICHARITO

BLUE PETERS BOLEYN TEVEZ BONDS

LONDON WEST HAM UNITED JOE HART NOBLE

BROOKING BUBBLES BILIC STRATFORD

OVER LAND AND SEA HAMMERS TWIST AND SHOUT

CLARET AND BLUE TEASERS!

Test your knowledge of West Ham United with our 20-question Hammers Quiz. Give yourself a point for each one you get correct. Answers can be found on page 59-61!

1. Who finished as West Ham United's leading goalscorer in the 2016/17 season?

2. Which Slovenian team provided the opposition for the first-ever competitive match at London Stadium on 28 July 2016?

3. Who scored West Ham United's first Premier League goal of the 2016/17 season?

4. Which player provided the cross for Michail Antonio to score the first Premier League goal in London Stadium history against AFC Bournemouth on 21 August 2016?

5. The Hammers did the Premier League double over three clubs in 2016/17. Swansea City was one, Burnley was the second, but who was the third?

6. West Ham United scored four goals in a single Premier League fixture just once in 2016/17. Who were the opposition?

7. Which player recorded the best pass-completion percentage – 87.6% - of any player making ten or more Premier League appearances in 2016/17?

8. Darren Randolph made 22 appearances to Adrian's 16 in 2016/17, but which goalkeeper kept more Premier League clean sheets?

9. Which player appeared in more Premier League fixtures (35) than any other West Ham United player in 2016/17?

10. The Hammers played against Seattle Sounders and which other club during their two-match pre-season tour to the United States?

11. Who was the only West Ham United player to be booked ten times in the Premier League in 2016/17? (Clue – He's also been booked more times than any Hammer in history!)

12. How many matches did West Ham United's longest Premier League unbeaten run last season?

13. Which player wore the No28 shirt during the 2016/17 season?

14. How many of West Ham United's 45 points did the team earn from away matches last season?

15. Which young Hammers loanee was voted Bradford City's Players' Player of the Season for 2016/17?

16. West Ham United's lowest home attendance of the 2016/17 season also represented the Club's all-time League Cup attendance record, but who provided the opposition?

17. Which FIFA World Cup winner made four appearances for West Ham United last season?

18. How many African players played first-team football for West Ham United in 2016/17?

19. Who was crowned Hammer of the Year in May 2017?

20. Which future Hammer scored the winner for Juventus in the Italian club's 3-2 Betway Cup win at London Stadium on 7 August 2016?

LONDON STADIUM

West Ham United moved into their iconic new London Stadium home in summer 2016, ending the Club's 112-year stay at the Boleyn Ground in nearby Upton Park.

London Stadium played host to the 2012 Olympic and Paralympic Games, at which Team GB's athletes and para-athletes wowed the world with their achievements.

Here, you can learn seven things you probably didn't know about the Hammers' new home...

1. THREE YEARS IN THE MAKING

Construction work on London Stadium began in spring 2008 and took less than three years to complete. It originally contained two tiers, 14 floodlight pylons and 80,000 seats, each of which was equipped with an LED lighting paddle to help paint amazing pictures during the Olympic Games!

2. MEDALS GALORE!

Team GB won an amazing 185 medals at the 2012 London Olympic and Paralympic Games! The Olympians won 65 medals (29 gold, 17 silver and 19 bronze), while the Paralympians won 120 (34 gold, 43 silver and 43 bronze).

3. 99 YEARS

West Ham United were named preferred bidder to become anchor concessionaire for London Stadium by the Olympic Park Legacy Company in December 2012 and agreed a 99-year lease in March 2013.

4. CHEIKHOU AT THE DOUBLE

West Ham United hosted Slovenian opponents NK Domzale in their first-ever fixture at London Stadium on Thursday 4 August 2016. Cheikhou Kouyate scored the first two goals, with Sofiane Feghouli also netting in a 3-0 UEFA Europa League third qualifying round victory.

5. OFFICIAL OPENING

West Ham United officially opened London Stadium as their new home on Sunday 7 August 2016. The new Bobby Moore and Sir Trevor Brooking Stands were unveiled ahead of the Betway Cup clash with Italian champions Juventus. Andy Carroll scored twice, but the visitors won 3-2.

6. CAPACITY

London Stadium has a seating capacity of 60,045 in pitch mode – which includes West Ham United matches and other sporting fixtures – and 79,990 in concert mode, when the pitch is covered over to allow spectators to get a better view of their favourite artists on stage!

7. IT'S NOT JUST FOR FOOTBALL!

London Stadium might be West Ham United's new home, but it's not just for football. Aside from London 2012, the venue has also played host to the Anniversary Games, IAAF World Athletics and Para Athletics Championships, the Great Newham Run, Race of Champions motorsport and musical concerts featuring the likes of AC/DC, Robbie Williams and Guns N' Roses.

VIC WATSON – WEST HAM'S GREATEST GOALSCORER

9 things you didn't know about the man who scored a Club-record 326 goals for West Ham United.

- Vic Watson was born in the village of Girton, just north west of the famous city of Cambridge, on 10 November 1897.
- West Ham United paid just £25 to sign Watson from non-league club Wellingborough Town in 1920!

- In 1923, Watson helped the Hammers overcome the disappointment of losing their first FA Cup final by firing them to promotion to the First Division for the first time.
- Watson scored 13 hat-tricks and four goals on three occasions during a Hammers career spanning 15 seasons and 505 matches.
- The striker netted a Club-record six goals in West Ham United's 8-2 First Division win over Leeds United on 9 February 1929.
- Watson scored on his England debut in a Home Championship draw with Wales in Cardiff in March 1923. In total, he managed four goals in five appearances for his country.
- His most-prolific season was 1929/30, when he scored 42 in 40 First Division matches to finish as the leading scorer in the top flight.
- Watson also netted eight goals in four FA Cup ties the same season and, of the 48 games he started, Watson scored in 37!
- Vic Watson returned to his home village to become a market gardener. He died in August 1988, aged 91.

CHICHARITO!

West Ham United signed a true footballing superstar when they brought Javier Chicharito Hernandez to the London Stadium in July 2017.

The Mexico striker netted regularly during spells with Guadalajara, Manchester United, Real Madrid and Bayer Leverkusen.

Here, we find out more about El Tri's all-time record goalscorer...

FACT FILE CHICHARITO

Born:
1 June 1988, Guadalajara, Mexico

Clubs played for:
Guadalajara, Manchester United, Real Madrid, Bayer Leverkusen

International: Mexico (96 caps, 48 goals)

Career Appearances/Goals: 346/136

Did You Know?
Chicharito has appeared for Mexico at six major tournaments – two FIFA World Cups, two FIFA Confederations Cups, one Copa America and one CONCACAF Gold Cup.

Won as a player
2 Premier League titles

1 Mexican Premier League title

1 FIFA Club World Cup

1 CONCACAF Gold Cup

1 FA Community Shield

Did You Know?
Chicharito means 'The Little Pea' in Spanish. The striker's father Javier Hernandez, who also played for Mexico, was known as Chicharo or 'The Pea'!

FORWARDS

ANDY CARROLL

DATE OF BIRTH: 6 JANUARY 1989
PLACE OF BIRTH: GATESHEAD, ENGLAND
HEIGHT: 1.93M
JOINED WEST HAM UNITED: AUGUST 2012 FROM LIVERPOOL
WEST HAM UNITED APPEARANCES: 110
WEST HAM UNITED GOALS: 30
DID YOU KNOW? ANDY CARROLL WON THE INAUGURAL CHAIRMEN'S PLAYER OF THE YEAR AWARD IN MAY 2013
FIFA17 RATING: 78

DIAFRA SAKHO

DATE OF BIRTH: 24 DECEMBER 1989
PLACE OF BIRTH: DAKAR, SENEGAL
HEIGHT: 1.84M
JOINED WEST HAM UNITED: AUGUST 2014 FROM FC METZ
WEST HAM UNITED APPEARANCES: 54
WEST HAM UNITED CLEAN SHEETS: 20
DID YOU KNOW? DIAFRA SAKHO FINISHED AS WEST HAM UNITED'S LEADING SCORER IN HIS DEBUT SEASON IN CLARET AND BLUE IN 2014/15
FIFA17 RATING: 76

CHICHARITO

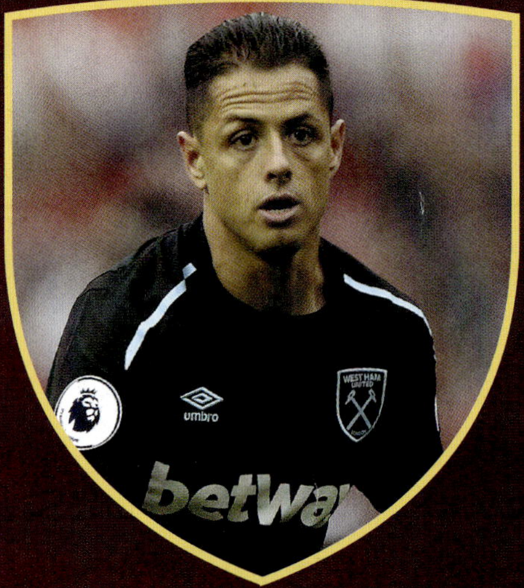

DATE OF BIRTH: 1 JUNE 1988
PLACE OF BIRTH: GUADALAJARA, MEXICO
HEIGHT: 1.75M
JOINED WEST HAM UNITED: JULY 2017 FROM BAYER LEVERKUSEN
WEST HAM UNITED APPEARANCES: 0
WEST HAM UNITED CLEAN SHEETS: 0
DID YOU KNOW? CHICHARITO TRANSLATES INTO ENGLISH AS 'LITTLE PEA'. HIS FATHER JAVIER HERNANDEZ WAS KNOWN AS CHICHARO, WHICH TRANSLATES AS 'THE PEA'
FIFA17 RATING: 83

ANDRE AYEW

DATE OF BIRTH: 17 DECEMBER 1989
PLACE OF BIRTH: SECLIN, FRANCE
HEIGHT: 1.76M
JOINED WEST HAM UNITED: AUGUST 2016 FROM SWANSEA CITY
WEST HAM UNITED APPEARANCES: 26
WEST HAM UNITED CLEAN SHEETS: 6
DID YOU KNOW? ANDRE AYEW HAS APPEARED AT TWO FIFA WORLD CUP FINALS AND FIVE AFRICA CUP OF NATIONS TOURNAMENTS FOR GHANA
FIFA17 RATING: 80

ANTONIO MARTINEZ

DATE OF BIRTH: 30 JUNE 1997
PLACE OF BIRTH: BARRIO DEL PROGRESO, MURCIA, SPAIN
HEIGHT: 1.8M
JOINED WEST HAM UNITED: JULY 2016 FROM VALENCIA
WEST HAM UNITED APPEARANCES: 0
WEST HAM UNITED CLEAN SHEETS: 0
DID YOU KNOW? ANTONIO MARTINEZ SCORED AGAINST BOTH MIDDLESBROUGH AND NEWCASTLE UNITED DURING OXFORD UNITED'S RUN TO THE 2016/17 FA CUP FIFTH ROUND
FIFA17 RATING: 61

NATHAN HOLLAND

DATE OF BIRTH: 19 JUNE 1998
PLACE OF BIRTH: WYTHENSHAWE, GREATER MANCHESTER, ENGLAND
HEIGHT: 1.8M
JOINED WEST HAM UNITED: JANUARY 2017 FROM EVERTON
WEST HAM UNITED APPEARANCES: 0
WEST HAM UNITED CLEAN SHEETS: 0
DID YOU KNOW? NATHAN HOLLAND SCORED THE FIRST-EVER NON-FIRST TEAM GOAL AT LONDON STADIUM WHEN HE NETTED AGAINST FULHAM IN FEBRUARY 2017
FIFA17 RATING: N/A

MATCH THE HAMMER TO HIS NATIONALITY!

West Ham United's first-team squad includes players from more than 15 different countries, but can you match the Hammer to his nationality?

Joe Hart

Adrian

Winston Reid

Jose Fonte

James Collins

Angelo Ogbonna

Arthur Masuaku

Cheikhou Kouyate

Sead Haksabanovic

Edimilson Fernandes

Martin Samuelsen

Manuel Lanzini

Andre Ayew

Chicharito

Marko Arnautovic

Answers on page 59-61

QUIZ AND PUZZLE ANSWERS

P10 SPOT THE DIFFERENCE 1

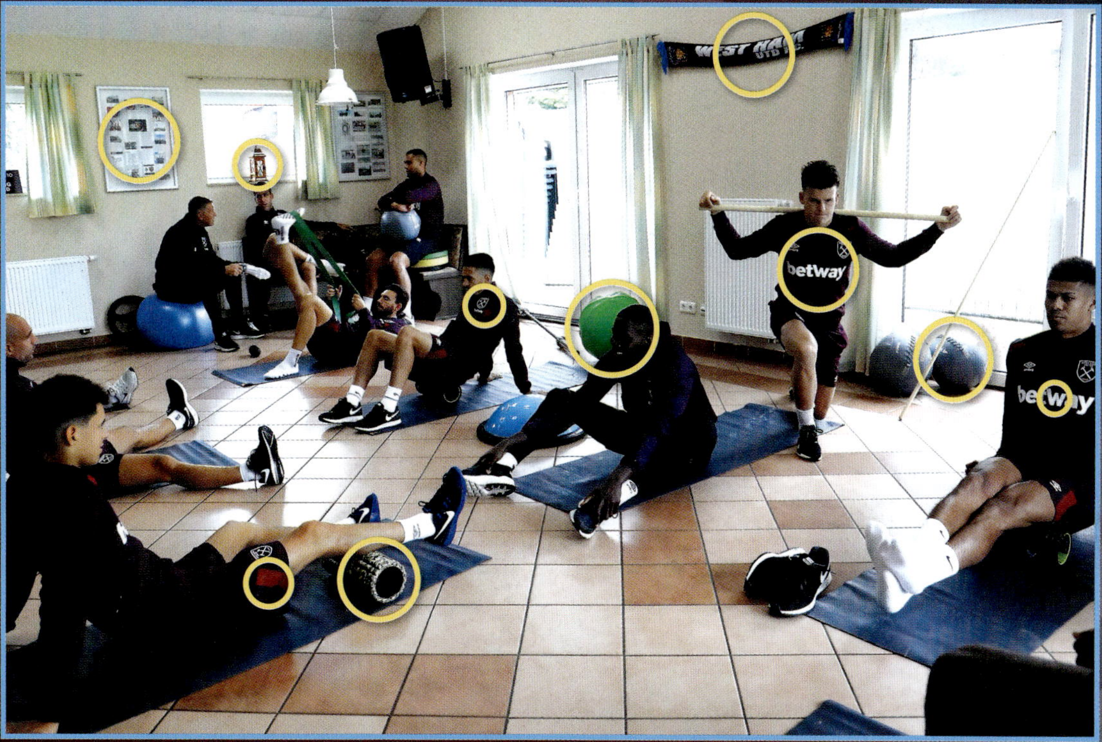

P11 CORNERED – PABLO ZABALETA

Where both answers are shown, he couldn't choose between the two options, so picked both!

SIRLOIN
NOEL GALLAGHER &
LIAM GALLAGHER
2012 PREMIER LEAGUE TITLE
CORONATION STREET
LIONEL MESSI &
SERGIO AGUERO
MANCHESTER DERBY
DIEGO MARADONA
GABRIEL BATITISTUTA
YAYA TOURE & KOLO TOURE
BOCA JUNIORS
CLEAN SHEET
ROBERT DE NIRO
JAVIER MASCHERANO

P18 NAME THE HAMMER – PICTURE QUIZ

1. Modibo Maiga
2. Mauro Zarate
3. James Tomkins
4. Alex Song
5. Stewart Downing
6. Marouane Chamakh
7. Joey O'Brien
8. Mohamed Diame
9. Emmanuel Emenike
10. Ricardo Vaz Te
11. Diego Poyet
12. Dimitri Payet
13. Jussi Jaaskelainen
14. Kevin Nolan
15. Simone Zaza

P21 CORNERED – AARON CRESSWELL

PS4
SUSHI
FERRARI
LOUISA JOHNSON
COFFEE
FA CUP WINNER
LIONEL MESSI
DOGS
INSTAGRAM
PELE
BEACH HOLIDAY
X FACTOR
KENNY DALGLISH
STEVEN GERRARD

P22-23 MATCH THE FACT TO THE HAMMER!

1. Joe Hart
2. Cheikhou Kouyate
3. Angelo Ogbonna
4. Robert Snodgrass
5. Sead Haksabanovic
6. Mark Noble
7. Manuel Lanzini
8. Aaron Cresswell
9. Arthur Masuaku
10. James Collins
11. Michail Antonio
12. Adrian
13. Edimilson Fernandes
14. Declan Rice
15. Andy Carroll
16. Andre Ayew
17. Jose Fonte
18. Ashley Fletcher
19. Pablo Zabaleta
20. Pedro Obiang

P36 SPOT THE DIFFERENCE 2

P49 WORDSEARCH

R	J	S	L	N	M	K	R	F	Z	M	Y	M	T	Z	L	W	D
Y	J	R	E	R	N	L	W	E	K	N	K	B	K	V	V	O	E
N	T	B	K	L	K	P	V	P	B	O	L	E	Y	N	N	V	T
F	U	R	B	R	B	E	N	O	B	L	E	R	L	B	M	E	I
M	O	O	V	S	T	B	P	Y	B	G	J	Q	R	T	G	R	N
V	H	O	N	N	T	J	U	K	T	L	J	B	V	D	F	L	U
K	S	K	P	K	M	R	T	B	C	R	U	G	D	J	Q	A	M
N	D	I	X	X	R	K	A	H	C	K	A	E	F	M	V	N	A
T	N	N	R	T	G	G	I	T	M	X	C	H	K	R	K	D	H
J	A	G	V	H	Z	C	N	R	F	P	E	T	E	R	S	A	T
H	T	H	F	H	H	N	E	R	O	O	M	N	J	O	L	N	S
J	S	V	G	A	O	S	D	K	F	P	R	F	L	M	J	D	E
J	I	C	R	D	R	I	B	Q	R	M	V	D	N	B	Z	S	W
P	W	I	N	E	C	W	O	Z	B	L	Y	M	H	K	T	E	F
R	T	O	M	A	I	H	N	N	Q	P	M	V	W	Y	K	A	Z
O	L	M	N	K	L	N	D	N	C	P	T	E	R	A	L	C	L
T	A	I	B	K	I	N	S	V	K	K	L	R	W	N	K	R	Z
H	O	M	N	L	B	P	F	B	L	B	D	R	R	T	Z	D	H

P50 CLARET AND BLUE TEASERS!

1. Michail Antonio
2. NK Domzale
3. James Collins v Chelsea (A), 15 August 2016
4. Gokhan Tore
5. Crystal Palace
6. 4-1 v Swansea City (A), 26 December 2016
7. Arthur Masuaku
8. Adrian (6) kept more clean sheets than Darren Randolph (4)
9. Manuel Lanzini
10. Carolina RailHawks
11. Mark Noble
12. Five (between 8 April-5 May 2017)
13. Jonathan Calleri
14. 20
15. Josh Cullen
16. Accrington Stanley
17. Alvaro Arbeloa
18. Four (Sofiane Feghouli, Cheikhou Kouyate, Diafra Sakho, Andre Ayew)
19. Michail Antonio
20. Simone Zaza

P58 MATCH THE HAMMER TO HIS NATIONALITY!

Joe Hart - England
Adrian - Spain
Winston Reid - New Zealand
Jose Fonte - Portugal
James Collins - Wales
Angelo Ogbonna - Italy
Arthur Masuaku - France
Cheikhou Kouyate - Senegal
Sead Haksabanovic - Montenegro
Edimilson Fernandes - Switzerland
Martin Samuelsen - Norway
Manuel Lanzini - Argentina
Andre Ayew - Ghana
Chicharito - Mexico
Marko Arnautovic - Austria

WHERE'S HAMMERHEAD?

Can you spot mascot Hammerhead celebrating Michail Antonio's goal with the West Ham United fans at London Stadium?